# My walk with God

By: Didi

# Table of Contents

## Introduction

My name is Didi, and I would like to invite you to take a peek into my walk with God. This short writing will be the first of the beginning of a series I like to call open discussions and its intentions are to be an example of ways we have been misled by the world and how we can get back on track.

In no way shape or form am I passing judgement on anyone, I have no room to do so in the eyes of the lord and would never attempt such behavior. Remember, everyone's walk with God will look different and God will convict us of different things at different times. Therefore, I would never expect you to follow along to the things I believe and have been convicted by God.

My only intention in this writing is to share my knowledge and education on the areas God has allowed me to improve in with the hopes and prayers of you receiving a much-needed blessing from the lord through these pages. Some of the writings in this book are my true personal convictions and others are what God chose to further educate me on. Most likely so that I could help others as he calls us to do in this world.

I have repeatedly prayed to the lord and asked him to make me into the woman of God he has designed me to be, and I have reasons to believe that this prayer was answered. Not everyone will understand my journey and why I had to make the decisions that were made and why I had to go where God sent me, but I like to believe it's for my own good and that is enough for me.

My open discussion series was designed with the idea of opening group discussions with other believers in Christ and talking about topics we may or may not hear in our church worship settings. I think it will be perfect for small groups, large groups, Sunday schools and bible studies. Purchase this writing with the intention of connecting with others inside the faith and maybe those who are not. Ask among yourselves some really tough questions and have meaningful deep discussions.

In the next column you will read about the discoveries I have come across and how I will approach life with these problems. I pray that each and every human being who reads this book discovers a true word from God and conviction in their hearts. I often wonder if we do enough to reach the kingdom of heaven or have we fallen into the ways of the world?

# The body God designed for me

**Romans 12:1-2**

**[1]** I beseech you therefore, brethren, by the mercies of God, that ye present your bodies a living sacrifice, holy, acceptable unto God, which is your reasonable service. **[2]** And be not conformed to this world: but be ye transformed by the renewing of your mind, that ye may prove what is that good, and acceptable, and perfect, will of God.

As a Christian, I read this scripture every day and I do the best I can to alternate my life around it in a way that Glorifies God. Because he accepts us as a part of him, I do not seek to harm his body which is the body he gave to me. I do my hardest to dissect in as many ways as possible and please God and not people.

Because I confess that I follow the lord and his ways, these are the practices I have adopted into my life concerning my body.

I will not alternate my physical appearance with False nails and polish, piercings, and tattoos, makeup and hair extensions and jewelry! In the past I had a collection of body piercings that became nothing except an obsession of how I thought they looked on me. When it was understood that I was crossing over into idolatry, I immediately removed them and have no desire to get them again.

I think to myself, God already designed me beautifully in his own image and I look good so why keep it covered? I felt like I was telling God that he didn't do a good job with my appearance and the blaring of that thought in my mind everyday became heavy.

Though I didn't wear much weave anyway, I vowed that I would continue to not wear it as well as false extension and nails. God didn't make anyone perfect and that's the beauty of it all.

After doing a lot of research, I not only felt as if I was covering Gods glory, I also thought to myself. You do not know what these products have to go through before they reach your body or hands, and you don't know what items are being prayed over and what's being preyed upon them. The possible evil that we are inviting into our lives could be the very items we are putting on our head for appearance or simply adding to our nails for attention.

The wearing of jewelry simply offers the opportunity for the Jezebel spirit to appear, and I simply do not want to carry that around. The spirit of the Jezebel seeks to control, manipulate, and deceive. It operates through seduction, deception, and manipulation through people's emotions. It is said in his word, anyone who acts like the jezebel spirit is not following Christ. (The engagement of immortality, idolatry, false teachings, and other repentant sins)

I am not professing that this happens to everyone who wears these items on their body. I am simply speaking for myself. Most of the items mentioned do not appeal to me or no longer do and because of it, I removed the weight of the items from my life. I know many do not understand because I am constantly questioned about why I don't do certain things, but everything is not for everyone. How dare I pray to my father in heaven and not put in the effort to change.

**James 2:26**

"What good is it, my brothers and sisters, if someone claims to have faith but has no deeds? Can such faith save them?"

For the glorification of God alone, I also practice minimalism in my wardrobe habits as well as modesty. This has had the best benefits for me, more than anything else I will talk about in this book. These two tools God has introduced me to, and it has saved my life from so much.

**Definition of modesty**

behavior, manner, or appearance intended to avoid impropriety or indecency.

**Definition of minimalism**

The promotion of being more intentional with every aspect of life and collecting what is most valuable and removing what is not.

I hold these tools dear to me so you may see them often in the books that I write because they were most helpful when God was removing me from depression. Because of my respect for God, modesty has become a daily practice that I stand firm in.

I love the body that God has gifted me with however I haven't always loved the way my body was treated. Unintentionally becoming the victim of sexual violation on more than one occurrence throughout my life has created deep anxiety and depression. The fear of being looked at as a sexual object at one point had taken over my mind. I was never big on showing my body anyway, but I became obsessed with trying not to look attractive or appear to anyone of the opposite gender as anything wanting to be noticed.

It drained my energy everyday as I searched for the perfect design that didn't make me as noticeable, I felt like nothing would work. I dressed more tomboyish hoping to not be seen and I still was but in a different way. Then people would say I was trying to be the opposite gender and it would just give me more anxiety because I knew it wasn't my intention and I never wanted to be as such.

The lord approached and got my attention and he let me know that it was okay to dress more respectfully because I am a representative for him, but it wasn't okay for me to fear his creation due to the actions of others. Slowly but surely, he took my focus from what was done to me and how to protect myself from it to how I can be more honoring to him.

**1 Peter 3:3-4**

Do not let your adorning be external—the braiding of hair and the putting on of gold jewelry, or the clothing you wear— but let your adorning be the hidden person of the heart with the imperishable beauty of a gentle and quiet spirit, which in God's sight is very precious.

## Discussions

Taking the challenge:

Take the necessary opportunity to set yourselves away from everyone else and truly focus on self-improvement. Not for the glorification of ourselves but for God. Allow God to isolate you for the sole purpose of reconnecting with him and stepping into the person he wants you to be. Dissolve your selfish desires and learn to walk where God tells you without questioning his authority!

It's not all bad, it's how we approach it that matters. Maybe God hasn't convicted you of the wearing of jewelry and false cosmetics and that's okay! Or maybe he has. God works on us in his own way and on his own time. I have no say so but following the reading above, let's ask ourselves some questions.

Q: What are new practices that could prevent or keep us from the jezebel spirit?

Q: Am I wearing these false cosmetics for the right reasons? Are they pleasing to God?

Q: Are the items I wear on my body representing the deceiving spirit which is the practice of those who implicate the jezebel spirit?

Q: How can I implicate modesty in my life? What benefits can come from using this tool in my everyday life?

Q: Can the practice of minimalism help you? How?

## Gluttony

A part of taking care of your body is not just making sure that you look presentable in the eyes of the lord, but we also have to be mindful of the things we invite inside of our bodies as well.

**What is gluttony?**

Gluttony is the enjoyment of excessive eating and drinking that has been disconnected from contentment in God.

Often, we pick and choose which sins we want to talk about and which ones we want to deal with, and the others are kept away from conversation and people's ears, but everything must come to light. I understand the desire and need of wanting to win people in your churches, but a church is no good unless the true word of God is being communicated completely and fully.

Our bodies are temples of God therefore we should care for them as a glory to him. That includes the food we eat and the amount we eat.

Ask yourselves this,

Q: the food that I eat, is God pleased with my habits?

Q: Should I be trying to do better and if so, how?

I am big on making a list, I think it is the most important thing you can do when you're learning. People who are the most successful are the ones who carefully plan in very much detail what they wanted and didn't want. Not only because I am a writer but simply because it frees my mind from so much wonder and chaos when I see my goals written in front of me.

I have never been the over eater because I was born with digestive discomfort, and it sometimes cause me graves of pain but over the years I have found myself eating unpleasing things mostly because I financially couldn't always afford my choice of food or because my ways were not accepted. I do encourage you to pay attention to what you are eating and how much of it you are consuming, then implicate the changes.

## Items I will not own as a Christian

As it says in his words, we are to live in this world but not be of it. Because of this I try not to live the way the world has accepted us to live. Not all things are pleasing to God, and I do believe that it is time to stop making excuses for the things that he instructs us not to be a part of, yet we are!

I am deep into the research of the identity and roots of everything I bring into my safe space and because of it, I have decided that these items mean me no well and are not pleasing in the eyes of the lord.

**Yoga paraphernalia**

In simplistic terms it's the practice, meditation and the worship of another God. The bible commands us to meditate on God's word however meditation practiced in yoga has a different meaning and motive that stands behind it and as Christ followers, our priority should be on our lord and savior Jesus Christ!

**1 peter 5:8**

[8] Be alert and of sober mind. Your enemy the devil prowls around like a roaring lion looking for someone to devour.

**What does it mean to meditate in the bible?**

To take some time and think about God and his word.

Most of these created practices come from eastern mysticism. We do not have to do something mystical or weird to get Gods attention. He hears our cries, and he will answer us on his terms not ours.

Yoga is over five thousand years old and is found in India. It was created to be a path to spiritual growth and enlightenment. The word yoga means union, it points to the union between your temporary self and God Brahman. Brahman is spiritual to energy, but he does not want a relationship with you.

I understand that some will argue that it is not harmful or if we add God into it then it fixes the problem but does it really? Yoga operates on the idea that you and God are one and it promotes self-worship.

**Healing stones or crystals**

According to crystal healers, the careful placing of crystals on a patient's body will align with their bodies and create healing. Some people use them to ward off bad energy or evil spirits. Others may use it for protection and signs for the attraction of wealth.

This is ungodly behavior and is the manipulation of the spirit world and is categorized as witchcraft. This item is also the practice of worshiping something other than the true God. How can you drink the lords cup and the devils cup too? The answer is you can't!

**Saint candles**

Catholics mostly engage in this practice, and they believe that they have friends in heaven who are the saints, and they have the freedom to communicate when in need. Though it seems nice to know that you have a friend in heaven, why can't you go straight to the father for yourself rather than asking for someone to talk to God for you. I'm not bashing anyone and their religion, I am simply referring to Christians.

**1 Timothy 2:5**

<u>5 For there is one God, and one mediator between God and men, the man Christ Jesus;</u>

## Sage for cleansing

Sage cannot protect you; it will not clean your home or your lives. The enemy is not afraid of your materialistic items that you use to so call keep him away, instead you are inviting him closer to your space.

God himself is the only protector and provider. You have to go to him and ask him for the same thing you assume these products will do. Give him all of the credit, he is a jealous God.

## Dream catchers

A dream catcher is a native American craft designed with the belief of protection from bad dreams and only inviting good ones in. However, I believe that this is just an invitation to inviting the devil in once again and being disrespectful to God.

## Astrology and zodiac paraphernalia

This is my favorite topic of them all only because this annoys me more than the others. Everywhere you go in today's culture, people ask you what your sign is, and it drives me insane to hear it. Especially when it falls from the lips of a professing Christian.

Do we not see the idolatry and idolization in the items I have named? Can we recognize the horrible demonic illusions that are being invited inside? The zodiac attempts to interpret the constellation of the stars in the sky and claims to predict the destiny of someone's life. Scripture explains to us that this is false and against

Gods command. Let the lord lead you, not to the following of these things.

I pray to my father for deliverance for his people who are hurting and have fallen into sin in which we did not know was practice of so. It doesn't hurt to look deeper into the origin of stuff and things before we invite them into our safe places.

# Celebrations I will not celebrate as a Christian

Though we will never reach perfection, it is in Gods will that we try our hardest to separate ourselves from the world we live in for our own good. As result, I have separated myself from the following celebrations or I've alternated my practice towards them. I pray the lord sees the hard work I have done to be closer to him and his word! Have you ever heard of the word paganism? Well, I will be bringing it up often in the next section of this writing and I will do my best to help you understand what it is and why I stay away from it.

According to the internet, Paganism is a term first used in the fourth century by early Christians for people in the Roman Empire who practiced polytheism, or ethnic religions other than Judaism. Paganism can lead to the ungodly practices if worshiped improperly. There are many different genres of paganisms and cannot be categorized in one sum of things. As we always do, we take what God meant for good and turn it into bad!

## Halloween

Halloween deceives to be fun and exciting for children and families and even Christians are participating. Kids dress up as idols, ghost and goblins lurk around, teens and adults gather and party, drinking and other sinful pleasures are being portrayed and witchcraft is being practiced. Halloween is dedicated to remembering the dead.

Okay the modern-day churches have alternated it into trunk or treat however I do not believe this to be enough and for this belief, I have removed this from my practice. Who are we really worshiping on this day? You are making the devil happy that Gods children gets the opportunity to celebrate him one day out of the year. Everyone has their own traditional practices, and they may not all seem damaging but the intention for the holiday remain the same.

**Easter**

Okay okay, I know what you are saying. Not celebrating the day God has risen! come on now but yes it has made the list and it is for good reason. In all cases it is not what you're celebrating, but it is how you celebrate. If you cannot celebrate responsibly then don't celebrate at all. I celebrate the resurrection of Christ and

I do it on more than just one day but especially on resurrection Sunday!

I will not practice the world's way though. It is unnecessary and yes, we may be having fun and the kids may have fun. However, it removes our attention from the true meaning of the celebration. It's not about the easter bunnies, eggs and candy but it is about Jesus and the rising he made over thousands of years ago for our benefits.

You may not feel the same way I feel about these practices, but I don't want to put my focus in the wrong things. All of the practices have some sort of paganistic practice, but you can successfully celebrate without feeling like your disrespecting God, it just takes hard work, personal conviction and patience for God to renew your minds. And when he does, you have to be willing to accept it!

**Valentines' day**

An ancient roman festival of fertility called Lupercalia was the valentines. Lupercalia which was celebrated on February 13th to 15th held pagan traditions that do not sit well with me when I think of the lord. Once again, it is the celebration of false Gods and bring on a world of trouble. I do not need a special day to show care for the ones I love, we should take time to do that every day. First, we must thank God for our loved ones and make sure we are not spreading idolatry.

**Christmas**

Did you know that December 25th is nowhere listed in the bible and is not a true representation of the day Jesus was born. I daily worship Jesus Christ and give thanks for his appearance and ultimate sacrifice without adding the found knowledge of scientists and their beliefs.

Christmas offers pagan traditions as well; our culture has caused us to believe in the worship of a Christmas tree. Something pagans were big on, and I do firmly believe it opens the door for the practice of idolization and the overconsumption of materialistic things. Are we really going to break our necks, wallets and our mental health over one day that is not even listed in the bible. Are we really going to risk our souls. My focus is the true worship of God, so I have moved these distractions from my life, and it has definitely been a huge benefit.

Not only all of this, we have been called to not celebrate our savior in tradition as the world's way of celebration. Instead of focusing on the practice of Christmas the way the world do things, I concentrate on my deep relationship with God by celebrating the holy days.

**Joshua 24:15**

[15] And if it seem evil unto you to serve the LORD, choose you this day whom ye will serve; whether the gods which your fathers served that were on the other side of the flood, or the gods of the Amorites, in whose land ye dwell: but as for me and my house, we will serve the LORD.

**Isaiah 47:13-14**

<sup>13</sup> All the counsel you have received has only worn you

out! Let your astrologers come forward,

those stargazers who make predictions month by month,

let them save you from what is coming upon you.

<sup>14</sup> Surely they are like stubble; the fire will burn them up.

They cannot even save themselves from the power of the

flame. These are not coals for warmth;  this is not a fire

to sit by.

**Isaiah 8:19**

<sup>19</sup> When someone tells you to consult mediums and

spiritists, who whisper and mutter, should not a people

inquire of their God? Why consult the dead on behalf of

the living?

**Deuteronomy 18:10-14**

[10] Let no one be found among you who sacrifices their son or daughter in the fire, who practices divination or sorcery, interprets omens, engages in witchcraft, [11] or casts spells, or who is a medium or spiritist or who consults the dead. [12] Anyone who does these things is detestable to the LORD; because of these same detestable practices the LORD your God will drive out those nations before you. [13] You must be blameless before the LORD your God.

## James 1:5

[5] If any of you lacks wisdom, you should ask God, who gives generously to all without finding fault, and it will be given to you.

## Mathew 24:24

<u>**24** For false messiahs and false prophets will appear and perform great signs and wonders to deceive, if possible, even the elect.</u>

# Why I practice minimalism and the connection to my faith

**Mathew 6-19:21NRSV**

<u>Do not store up for yourselves treasures on earth, where moth and rust consume and where thieves Break in and steal. For where your treasure is, there your heart will be also.</u>"

From the beginning of our lives, we are taught that we cannot survive everyday life without the collection of material items. When we bring a child into the world, we prepare to consume a multitude of supplies and sometimes we do not use them often or even at all.

We watch social media, and we allow people behind a camera to tell us what we need or should buy for our environment. We allow our families to convince us that we do not have enough. Have you ever been introduced to minimalism? Do you know what it is?

Joshua Becker identifies and defines minimalism as the intentional promotion of the things we most value and removing everything that distracts us from it. As a Christian I genuinely believe that minimalism can be a remarkable thing when it comes to our mental health and relationship with God. Because of our addiction to overconsumption or materialistic things, we down those who have little to nothing. Let me just say to those who do not have a lot, you have just enough. There is nothing wrong with that. We fail as humans when we do not include someone for not having material items, we also create a world of troubles for the individual.

I am sure we make them feel down causing them to mentally and emotionally hurt themselves to meet society's expectations of a good life. Who do you want to live for God or the world? I would rather receive my treasures in heaven than on earth. STOP allowing society to pray on your weakness and insecurities.

The word that I want to bring to your attention is minimalism! As I have mentioned above, minimalism is practicing intentionality within every or many aspects of our lives. I know that some people are turning the found word minimalism into an esthetic but if it is carefully approached the correct way, it can be a success and, in our faith, it can help us grow in the lord. Though there are important questions you must ask yourself.

Q: Do I want to be a true follower of Christ? Am I willing to follow his lead?

Q: Do you want to be a part of society, or do you want to be a part of God?

I love the approach of this idea; however, society has once again turned something good into something bad or a sin.

Getting back to natural living and being as close to God is my true heart's desire in life. I do not want the enemy to destroy me as he approaches to attempt. Slowly but surely, I constantly ask myself over and over, what do I really need? What should I really do?

Minimalism looks different for all of us, so no judging or bullying others for not looking like you.

My entire life, I have fought and struggled with heavy depression, anxiety, and the repeated thoughts of suicide. After being told what to do and realizing I mentally could not complete what was expected of me, I thought that I was broken, and I wasn't worth anything except to be nonexistent.

I always knew I was consumed with too many things, and I knew it had something to do with what was wrong with me. I just did not know how to name it. Only recently discovering that I am not the one who is broken, but the world is. I boldly stand behind my decision to live the way that I have been living regardless of this world trying to place me somewhere I do not want to be and know I don't want to be.

I have honestly tried life the world's way and it does not work at all for me. The world says that we must have certain things in life, or we are nothing, but we are more important when we have less.

After living in more than one apartment in my early adulthood, I listened to people tell me what I needed and how much I needed and so many times I wanted to get rid of everything I had and just have a big empty room. At the time I did not know I could do it. I was so busy listening to my peers tell me what I should be doing with my life and the constant nag of telling me what I was doing wrong.

I finally did official destruction. The ultimate cry out to God that was much needed. A plea that he would save me from worldly desires and set my eyes and heart on him only. Shortly after, he did just that. In the beginning I was afraid of the way things looked but I freely walk with no problem with the way things look. I figured I had walked on faith before so why not do it again. Why not do it every day of my life.

I say to him LORD remove the material I do not need and that is sinful in your eyes. LORD my God I ask that you make me into the true woman of God that you need me to be. So, he did, he has removed so much, and I have been feeling so much better. I do not miss the items I had. Once I got over the desires of the flesh through material items, I began to go through what is called a withdrawal. Often feeling like a drug addict overcoming a drug.

The benefits of this tool have been nothing but a true blessing, but I say it requires constant learning, researching and improvement.

**What is minimalism?**

According to Joshua Becker the definition of minimalism is the intentional practice of promotion of the things we most value and removing everything that distracts us from it. My understanding of this tool is to dig deep into the true meaning of life and collect what is most meaningful and let nothing or no one stand in your way from the pleasure it brings into your life. Removing the things that bring us no meaning and joy and focusing on what is important.

Having materialistic items is not a sin nor is it a dreadful thing. Though, having too many materialistic possessions may be concerning for your mental, physical, emotional and spiritual health. Since the beginning of time, the beginning of your life the lesson that has been taught and improvised is that we need stuff. But do we really? When preparing for a child to enter the world, we buy or have been gifted a multitude of material items. Sometimes more than we know what to do with. I will not compare us to Christ but will use him as an example. Jesus walked this earth with truly little and was successful!

Advertisements from popular companies, social media influences and society in general pray on your weakness and convince you that you do not own enough or what you have isn't good enough until you get their products. The media tells you to buy the newest, latest thing on the market. Only to tell you months later to get rid of it and get their most recent product.

Christ called us to live in this world but not be of it, yet as proclaiming Christians we do the exact opposite. Why? Are we trying our hardest to fit in with the world's way so that we do not feel out of place? God has given us permission to be different and out of cultural normality. How dare we not follow his command? Can't you see that this world is filled with the enemy, and he has come to attack? Why are we letting him?

The overconsumption of stuff and things has also made some of us nasty human beings. We beat each other down for the thing's others do not have and can't afford and ignore people and their cries for help because of their appearances, what they have and don't have. Who have we become? Even the believers in Christ.

Minimalism cannot save nor heal you however this God given tool can be used to bring you closer to him. If used properly. I can honestly account for him using this tool to bless and save me every day of my new life with Christ.

There was a time in my life where I began to fall apart and was suffering mentally. I have a sincere heart for my family and friends, but I felt sick when I was given things. I didn't feel free at all, even when it may have seemed as if I were. I was battling depression, anxiety, and suicidal thoughts until I went to Jesus himself and asked sincerely for his heart.

When I was a child, I had a hard time keeping my personal area clean and it spilled into adulthood. Not that I wanted to be that way, but mentally I couldn't do it. Because I couldn't, I often got in trouble for not completing the task that was asked of me. It made me feel like I was a horrible person, and I didn't know how to explain to people that I wanted to clean but mentally I just couldn't.

I was overwhelmed by the number of things I had and the many decisions I had to make for each individual item in my collection. So many times, I thought to myself I really wish I could throw everything away and just have a big empty room. It was not until I pleaded with God to save my life from the destruction, I was bringing upon myself that I was beginning my healing.

I ask him to break me from the danger I was bringing me into my own life and make me into the woman of God he needed me to be. Shortly after he led me to where I needed to be. I am huge on research, writing and searching. I am always questioning something in life. Though I use social media to communicate with friends and family, I use my devices for studying and researching and sometimes I must use media to find my answers or to build an understanding.

I am often watching videos of different topics and using my bible and devotions to confirm the information that is being taught to me. It took me months to dive deep into the true understanding of what minimalism is, how it applies to Gods word and what the worlds' view of this word or tool is. The only way to identify your priority of this word, you must understand it. He used this to help me, and I want to share it with you.

At first, I didn't know I was allowed to go without less. The world around me constantly told me that I didn't have enough. Although I was stressed about all my items, I was listening to family and friends when they told me what I needed. Then I realized that I didn't need all those things to have a comfortable life.

## The Livingroom

I carefully noticed that I often find myself sleeping or sitting on the floor. Even with a nice bed and sofa, I still ended up on the floor. As a direct result of my understanding about myself and realizing that I have been that way my whole life and that it's most likely not going to change, I decided to no longer buy or use furniture.

I was born with scoliosis and spinal bifida, I have always had a demanding time finding the perfect mattress and chair and after going through so many products I discovered that it was nothing that truly made me feel good throughout the night. I have never been able to sleep a full night on a bed which gave me the idea to eliminate the furniture item completely. Yes, that is right! no sofa, no coffee table. I do have a table though it is used for multiple things. It is not only saving me money from buying what I really do not use but it is saving me time from having an extra item I must clean. This one foldable table is used as my coffee table, writing table, desk and so many more things. There is no need for five tables in one room. I chose to invest in items that are not for individual use and quality as well as manageable.

You may not agree with my method, but it works for me. This works perfectly for me because I want to reconnect with naturalism as much as possible. Did you know that our bodies were not designed for the multiple structures such as chairs and beds that we add to our homes? I'm religiously into the holistic approach of everything. God gave us natural tools to help us, yet modern society has allowed us to forget what he gave us.

I have invested in small minimal furniture such as a cushion to sit on and a floor table that serves as a multitude of things.

Q: Why do we need a coffee table and side tables?

Q: Are we keeping these furniture items clean?

The floor table that I have invested in has cut down my cleaning time a lot, especially because of its unique design. It folds into a smaller table and can be stored away easily after being wiped down gently with a light product. I am no longer stressed about the number of items that I have and not being able to clean everything the way it should be.

## The Wardrobe

I found myself overwhelmed with the many materials peace's I had in my wardrobe and often drove myself mentally crazy on wash day only because I never got the task completed. At this point I just assumed I am such a disgusted and horrible person because I cannot seem to finish anything involving making my space look normal.

Normally, my clothes would be everywhere across my home, and it would usually take me months to pick them up. There was never anything wrong with my hands as to why I could not clean up but there was something wrong with my brain. Sometimes people deal with being depressed to the point where they could not even get out of bed, or they would experience a panic attack. I was that person!

A method I have created to help me with the size of my wardrobe is the 10-rule method. Instead of having three hundred pieces of cheap material in my wardrobe, I have decided to sacrifice quality over quantity, and I took honor in my most worn possessions. One day I came into my house, and I did a huge giveaway. I pulled out every single clothing item I had, and I made a pile from the clothes I hardly wore, to the clothes I wear sometimes to the clothes I wear every day and I concluded that I wore extraordinarily little compared to what I had.

Q: Do you need a closet with one hundred pairs of black shoes and nine hundred pairs of clothing items?

It is time for us to detach from our relationship with stuff and get back to the true purpose of life and that is God. Have you ever heard of the phrase; our stuff makes us sick? Well, it is true! The constant consumption of materialistic items has often affected our mental health as well as our physical health. I am not saying that you must go and throw away everything and have absolutely nothing.

Find the items that are most purposeful to you and remove the items that are not. I honestly do not even think I have 10 items but that was the goal I was trying not to exceed. When I sat down and processed my lifestyle, I took into consideration that I barely wear anything number one because I am not a huge clothing person.

Because I have sensitive skin and I have had a multitude of surgeries throughout my life, clothes sometimes irritate my skin and often cause infections after being worn for an extended period of time so as much as possible, I try not to wear much. When I am in the comfort of my home, I wear a pair of shorts, a sports bra, and my long robe. Even when I am cold, I am still wearing the same thing because I own a heating blanket for when I am on the chill side.

Q: If we wear the same things, why do we need all the other things?

Not only have I limited the items, but I have also limited the color of my wardrobe. Though I love wearing colors, they give me anxiety and they began to fill overwhelming to deal with, especially when it is time to wash them. As a result, I only wear the color black! It is not only simple but because I work at a place where my uniform is black with the company's logo on it, it just makes it so much easier. An easy task to wash clothes now, I only have little to wash, and everything is one color. No need to separate my laundry for the protection of the color and the anxiety of not being able to clean on the basis of the world's standards.

It has definitely taken away decision fatigue which has given me a clearer mind. I now have more time to focus on the things that truly matter rather than spending it cleaning and being tired and overwhelmed.

## The kitchen

I became attracted to the idea of an all-in-one item, and I am hooked. Americas kitchens look insane and cluttered with unnecessary goods that mean us no good. Why do we need a microwave, crock pot, stove, blender, chopper, hand mixer and pressure cooker in one kitchen? Yes, all these products individually have their niches and can be used for good, but do we need that many.

I am not promoting the idea that you specifically copy my style of design, but you can take something from it. Before purchasing the items, I chose for my kitchen, I carefully studied and did extensive research on the identity of the item. Then I allowed it to sit in my online shopping cart account for one full year and throughout that year I continued to ask myself if I still need it, what would I need it for, would I use it, or will it be in storage and why would it benefit my life. By the end of the year my needs outwaited my wants and desires and I prayed and gave myself permission to make the purchase if it was suitable.

I chose an all-in-one air fryer that serves as my toaster oven, microwave, oven, dehydrator, roaster, air fryer etc. Yes, that one machine that does all those things and more in one. Yes, one item that sits on my countertop. I Also did the exact same thing when it came to choosing a blender also made by the same company and is an all in one. Chopper, blender, dough maker, ice cream maker etc. Also, the designs are very simple and non-bulky. Because of this method I am saving countertop space and my money as well. Just two items and many functions between them both.

I have downsized my dinnerware down to the simple

2 large bamboo sectional trays

1 glass bowl with handle and top

And one silverware set (Fork, Knife, Spoon)

For drinking I use my oversized yeti that's 64 oz and a glass tumbler that is 36 oz.

I have one extra cup from the company that I work for that I use as extra or for guest!

I am sure you may be wondering, well if I take away my variety of items then are you creating more work for yourself? The answer is yes, no, and there is a very important reason why the answer yes exists. I use one kitchen item at a time, and I clean it immediately after using. As for my clothing materials, I use what is called an air dresser to refresh my clothes everyday instead of repeatedly washing them back-to-back. If it does not show stains or smell bad then I will not wash it, I will use the dresser to refresh it for the next use.

Those are just a few examples of minimalism improving my life for the good. You may be asking right about now, what does this have to do with God and getting closer to him. Well let me explain.

Q: Why do we need so many things? Why have we as Christians allowed this world to stray us away?

**What are the advantages of practicing minimalism? (Christian perspective)**

1.  We bring sickness, hard ache, and pain to ourselves sometimes through our compulsive addictions and behaviors. Decreasing the amount of time, we spend trying to get our environments in a set order will not only remove the stress but free your time for what is more important.

2.  It can decrease the wear and tear that we place on our bodies when we are trying to force ourselves to do so much at a time. Should it really take us a full day or more to get our place in order? The less we have, the less we must care for!

3.  Focusing on our new selves and the things we will not do anymore such as buying insane amounts of products can financially benefit us

eventually and allow us to save money for what is most important. It will help us control our impulses and fleshly desires when we take the time to understand what habits are wrong and how to overcome them.

4. It decreases our chances of developing the spirit of Idolatry and if we have already, we now could remove it from our lives.

5. You have been using your material belongings as a separation from God without realizing. I cannot talk to God right now because I must wash my clothes! I am unable to read my bible now because I must go wash my dinnerware or clean my room and it's going to take me most of the day!

6. The possessions we carry once weighed us down but no longer have too. I do believe that our items we carry hold burdens and sometimes pain that God wants us to give to him and let him take care of

7. The benefits of owning less and taking care of the little that I have can also represent to God that I am not lazy which sometimes we do because of our items. I have seen many try this. When they are out of clean clothes, instead of washing the ones they already have, we add to our consumption and makes us lazy. Yes we are hardworking, and I am sure some of us try our hardest, but we are not perfect, and I am not holding you to that standard.

I hope that you were able to follow along and understand the message that God is trying to bring to you. He wants you to come to him and focus on what he has for us that is most important. Your children for example, pay attention to them and hear them out while you can. Before you know it, they will all be grown, and you do not want to feel like you've missed out on their childhood. Spend time getting closer to God, understand his word and do his works. Reach out to your community and give back as God has commanded of us.

## Discussions

Taking the challenge:

I challenge us to use minimalism to reconnect with God, our friends and family. Reconnect with ourselves, and nature overall. I am not suggesting that you go full on Amish, however I am encouraging you to use this tool to decide what is blocking you from the true goals in life.

Go into your house and pray to your father in Christ! Pray that God leads you and protects you from the sin you did not even know was sin. Pray for the lord to convict you of the things you need to let go of. Pray for the convictions of the people, places, and habitual habits you need to remove! The only way to improvement is the personal convictions of God.

Go through your stuff, make piles. Let's get things truly in the order they should be in. Pull out everything in front of you. Grab a pen and paper and make a list. While making that list, ask yourself and answer these important questions.

Q: What items do I really need? What items do I most value and why?

Q: How many of these items do I really need? Do I really need extras for guests? Do I often entertain guests, or should I discard the decluttered item?

Q: what items in my environment is less pleasing to God? What is pleasing to God?

Q: How does this glorify God?

Q: Is this item damaging to my health?

Q: Why do I hold on to such earthly treasures and why

does it bring me pleasures?

# A woman's convictions from the LORD

As a woman of the highest God, I put my concentration into being the best woman I can be for him, and I believe that he has made changes in me. I Have always been reserved and off to myself so some of these changes were not as hard and others may have been. Last year I asked my peers a question on my social media platform for the research and purpose of this book. I asked what is the definition of a woman?

Boy where the reactions mixed and all over the place. Let me introduce to you the characteristics of a woman of God. These are my notes that I want to share with you. This topic is for the men as well. Women who show these behaviors habitually are the women that should catch your attention if you are a true believer in Christ.

1. **To be a godly woman, you are to love God with all of your heart.**

   **Mathew 22:37**

"Jesus said unto him, Thou shalt love the Lord thy God with all thy heart, and with all thy soul, and with all thy mind."

How do we show our love to God?

- Follow his commandments and not the ways of the world
- Seek him and his words at all times

2. **To be a Godly woman you must love your neighbor as you love yourself**

**Mathew 22:39**

[39] And the second is like it: 'Love your neighbor as yourself.'

What are ways we can demonstrate our love for our neighbors?

- Love people, even when they hurt you. Pray for them when they hurt you or others
- Help them even when they are talking about you
- Love your family, even when they do wrong by you

3. **A Godly woman is full of wisdom and kindness**

**Proverbs 31:26**

She speaks with wisdom, and faithful instruction is on her tongue.

How can we show kindness? What is wisdom?

- Being respectful and use manners

Wisdom is having knowledge and understanding how to apply it to our lives. (Living biblically)

## 4. Godly women are merciful and forgiving

### Micah 6:8

He has shown you, O mortal, what is good. And what does the LORD require of you? To act justly and to love mercy and to walk humbly with your God.

What does merciful mean? How do we demonstrate forgiveness?

Being merciful is exercising forgiveness and passion for others

- It is important to understand what forgiveness is and what it is not
- Consider why you want to forgive (for flesh or for God?)

- Take the appropriate opportunity to process your emotions

- Develop the mindset of forgiveness

- Practice forgiving (say I forgive!)

**5. Godly women demonstrate humility**

What is humility?

- Humility is the fear of the LORD

- Submission to authority without personal pride

How do we practice humility? (Modesty of the mind)

- Let others speak (accept feedback)

- Do not pry

- Look on the bright side (admiration)

- Accept being disappointed sometimes

- Ignore the negative actions of others (pray for them)

- Being okay with people not liking you

- Back down from useless fights

- Always be polite

- Be grateful

- Complement others

- Apologize for your mistakes

- Ask for help

- Self-compassion is important

# The filtration of my life

Speaking of the idea of stepping away from the world's ways, I have used some of the previous techniques to deal with the convictions concerning my life. I mentioned before that we must be careful of the things we invite into our bodies and personal environments. That also include our eyes and ears!

Understanding that we cannot control everything we see and everything that we hear but there are some things that we do have control over.

### ***Entertainment***

What is entertainment?

The action of providing or being provided with amusement or enjoyment.

Examples of entertainment can include but are not limited to,

**Exhibition entertainment**

- Amusement parks
- Art shows
- Museums

**Live entertainment**

- Circus
- Clubs
- Comedy clubs
- Sporting events

**Mass media entertainment**

- Films
- Music

- Choirs

- Books

- Bands

## Electronic entertainment

- Video games

- SMS Content

- Toys

I will say this again, these items are not all representation of bad and evil, but our human natural will find a way to identify them as such.

Q: Has entertainment become a source of idolatry in your life?

Q: Has the consumption of these types of entertainment become compulsive for you?

Q: The entertainment that you are consuming on a daily basis, is it taking you away from God?

Q: what type of entertainment is being implicated in what you are watching and listening too?

I am a huge music person, compulsively! Only because I love to sing mostly. I was the girl in high school with a large playlist of over thousands of songs downloaded on my device. I personally did not care if my phone had service or not! As long as I had my music, was okay! I had my music organized in a multitude of playlists and had backup copies on more than one device in case I needed to redownload.

Christian music, rap music, r&b music, Hip Hop, Spanish, you name it, I had a playlist for it. I thought I could not be without my music because in certain moments it was enjoyable to me. It was the very first thing I remember God convicting me on. I do not fully understand why God had to bring me all of the way to Florida to convict me though. He needed me out of my comfort zone and shy box!

I heard him clear as day, "those rough, inappropriate, disrespectful words mean you no good and are keeping you for me." I thought I was doing good because at least I listened to my Gospel on a regular. Mostly because I was in the choir and had to find new songs for my performances.

Oh, he destroyed me with this one! At first I thought he was explaining to me that I was not allowed to listen to music at all and it was a big ouch for me. Until he directed me to my largest learning tool of all on my device. With the direction of God, I used YouTube to discover the deepness and poison behind the things I once valued going into my ear and were playing on full blast. It was hard to accept but for the lord I am willing to do anything to the best of my ability and I knew I could do it.

After extensive research and note-taking, I dashed into my Amazon Music playlist and sadly but gracefully deleted 4,297 songs of all genres including my Christian/Gospel playlist because it is not only what you listen to but the identity of what you're listening too. As much of a hurt this was for me I am here to say that my entertainment has become clean of the things that do not glorify the LORD.

I am sure I must explain How worship music was removed from the list as well and I will in a much explanatory way. Understand that we are human and

Christian media is created by human! We will never be perfect but in the things we listen to and watch especially Christian content, we must do our homework and we must know and understand the bible!

I am sorry that I have to break the news to you, but I must do so for it will be beneficial to you, ***all Christian commentary and content are not aligned with scripture!*** You have to get it in your minds, I'm not saying all, but an amount of our public figures I gospel and Christianity do not produce content that identifies and aligns with the word of God! Check the theology behind the music you bob your heads too and play in your churches at worship services.

Unfortunately, but fortunately, I had no choice except to remove a lot of songs from my playlist, repent for listening to them and consuming such false doctrine as well as pray for those that know not what they do is blasphemy in the eyes of the LORD. It is not only the music but the tv shows, books and so many more entertaining resources! I am certain that I just crushed someone's spirit for this one but some of our favorite celebrity pastors with all of the money and books, videos and motivational speeches are included when I say that they are not teaching from the bible.

## Mathew 7:21

[1] "Not everyone who says to me, 'Lord, Lord,' will enter the kingdom of heaven, but only the one who does the will of my Father who is in heaven.

Though in secular world entertainment it is most often obvious to one's eyes, in our Christian content, we may not always recognize or know. Remember, because it has Christian, Gospel or worship in its title do not make it biblical content.

# Closing View

My overall point of view is that I do not feel we try our hardest to be better human beings, better Christians. I believe in deeply searching for the beginning of everything and understanding the roots and history so that we will have a better understanding of what we are practicing.

We have easily fallen into the world's way without even realizing it. We make excuses for so many wrongs that God himself has told us in his word of which he does not approve. This writing is only my convictions and advice to all of my fellow brothers and sisters in Christ, not a demand. I would love to see everyone make it out of this world and to our true kingdom in heaven which requires a lot of hard work and faith.

I pray that you have enjoyed this short tour of a portion of my journey with God. Enjoy your day and grow in the LORD.

If it became obvious to readers that I was short and straight to the point in this writing, first let me apologize and further explain my actions. I did it intentionally with the sole purpose of leaving the long extended detailed version for a book I will release later for other intentions.

# Gratitude

I would like to give gratitude to all of you for taking the time and the opportunity to gain experience something new and accept Gods teachings through these pages. I thank everyone who has participated in your personal growth and development as well as my own.

To all who used their hard earned money to purchase a copy of this writing, I am most grateful, and I Give God thanks for all of you! Thank you to all who offered physical, emotional, and financial support.

I want you to know that you by purchasing a copy of my work you have not only made my dream come true, but you have allowed me to further believe in the gift God has given to me and I promise to continue using it to glorify our father in heaven God almighty!

## Proverbs 18:16

[16] A gift opens the way and ushers the giver into the presence of the great.

Most honorably, I give the highest thanks to God! You did all things for me and there was nothing I could do without you! Thank You!

Thank you!

# Acknowledgements

As mentioned earlier, I spent many hours doing research to assure I give you the best knowledge as I possibly could, and it wouldn't be right of me if I didn't give credit to where I received some of my knowledge and education from.

Because I am a visual learner, most of my extensive information was studied from my favorite Christian youtubers and digital content. I have reason to believe that they wouldn't mind me publicly thanking them for doing as the LORD has laid on their individual hearts and because of this I was able to receive the information that God needed me to pay attention to so that I could do his work and his will

**YouTube References:**

Jessica Joy

DLM Christian Lifestyle

Grace for purpose

Treasure Christ

Vladhungrygen

Got questions Christian's ministries

Fight for truth

Joshua Becker

**Other references:**

Discovery History

The Holy Bible KJV

Gateway bible NIV, KJV, NKJV

You version Bible application and website

And most importantly, God the father!

Made in the USA
Columbia, SC
21 December 2023

29146615R00055